On the _____ day of _____ ,

in the year of Our Lord _____ ,

in the Christian Community of _____ ,

located in

_____

_____

shared fully in the Eucharistic Celebration

by receiving Holy Communion

_____

We Celebrate the Eucharist

We Cel the Eu the Celebrate

This program also includes a Catechist's Guide, Family Guide, Program Director's Manual, Celebrations Book, and Record.

celebrate
eucharist

We Celebrate the Eucharist

Christiane Brusselmans

Christiane Brusselmann

Brian A. Haggerty

Brian A. Haggerty

Silver Burdett

MORRISTOWN, NJ

SILVER BURDETT & GINN

Acknowledgments

Excerpts from *The New American Bible*,
© Confraternity of Christian Doctrine 1970,
are used by permission of the copyright owner.

English translation of excerpts from
*Eucharistic Prayers for Masses with Children and
for Masses of Reconciliation.* Copyright © 1975,
International Committee on English in the Liturgy, Inc.
All rights reserved.

English translation of excerpts from the *Roman Missal.*
Copyright © 1973, International Committee on English in the
Liturgy, Inc. All rights reserved.

Photo Credits
viii: Silver Burdett. x: t.l. David Austen/Stock, Boston;
b.l. Jeffrey Reed/The Stock Shop; t.r., b.r. Michal Heron
for Silver Burdett. xi: t. © Jeff Apoian/Photo
Researchers, Inc.; b.l. Silver Burdett; t.r. Dan De Wilde
for Silver Burdett; b.r. Eugene Luttenberg/Art Resource.
xii: l. Silver Burdett; r. Dan De Wilde for Silver Burdett. l:
Burk Uzzle/Magnum. 10: l. Roger Malloch/Magnum; r.
Burk Uzzle/Magnum. 11: l. Silver Burdett; r. Eugene
Luttenberg/Art Resource. 20: l. Silver Burdett; r. Burk
Uzzle/Magnum. 21: l. Dan De Wilde for Silver Burdett; r.
Silver Burdett. 30: l. Jeffrey Reed/The Stock Shop; r. Burk
Uzzle/Magnum. 31: Burk Uzzle/Magnum. 40: l. Silver
Burdett; r. Burk Uzzle/Magnum. 41: Burk Uzzle/Magnum.
50: l. John Running; r. Dan De Wilde for Silver Burdett.
51: l. Burt Glinn/Magnum; r. Harald Sund. 60: l. Tom
Myers; r. Burk Uzzle/Magnum. 61: l. Andrew Sacks/
Art Resource. r. C. Tucker/Taurus Photos. 70: Burk Uzzle/
Magnum. 71: l. Michal Heron for Silver Burdett; r. David
Austen/Stock, Boston. 80: l. Michal Heron for Silver
Burdett; r. Silver Burdett. 81: l. Hiroji Kubota/Magnum; r.
© Jeff Apoian/Photo Researchers, Inc. 92: Silver Burdett.

Katherine R. Wood, at the age of six,
did the hand-lettering
on the cover
and throughout the book. *Katherine R. Wood*

The art is by
Monique Piret Weyers. *Monique Piret Weyers*

Hardcover edition   ISBN 0-382-00301-2

Softcover edition   ISBN 0-382-00375-6

Nihil obstat

Nihil Obstat:
Reverend Anselm Murray, O.S.B. *Censor Librorum*

Imprimatur

Imprimatur:
✠ Most Reverend Frank J. Rodimer Bishop of Paterson
June 3, 1983

The *nihil obstat* and *imprimatur* are official declarations
that a book or pamphlet is free of doctrinal and moral error.
No implication is contained therein that those who granted
the *nihil obstat* and *imprimatur*
agree with the contents, opinions, or statements expressed.

The contents and approach of the We Celebrate the Eucharist
program are in accord with *Basic Teachings for Catholic
Religious Education* issued by the National Conference
of Catholic Bishops, the *General Catechetical Directory*
issued by the Sacred Congregation for the Clergy,
and *Sharing the Light of Faith, National Catechetical Directory
for Catholics of the United States* issued by the
United States Catholic Conference.

Contents

Dear Family,
Preparing to receive the Eucharist
for the first time can be one of the most memorable
experiences you will share with your child. This gold book
represents a special invitation to you to help support and guide your child
on the journey to first reception of the Eucharist.

You are not alone on your journey. We invite you to join with other families, catechists,
priests, and parish members in this privileged task. Because of the love you
have for your child, we ask you to participate, as only
you can, in this sacramental preparation.

This book belongs to your child. It is truly a "golden book" because it will introduce the presence
of Jesus in a deeper way and show how we celebrate this presence in the Eucharist. You
and your child will discover beautiful pictures, stories of Jesus from the
Bible, prayers that you can share with all God's family when you
join with them in church.
You will find pages on which your child's personal stories can be drawn or
written. Great care will be invested in these pages. The fruit of
this experience will be offered to Jesus on your child's
First Communion Day.

We wish you God's joy and peace as you
begin on your way to the Table
of the Lord!

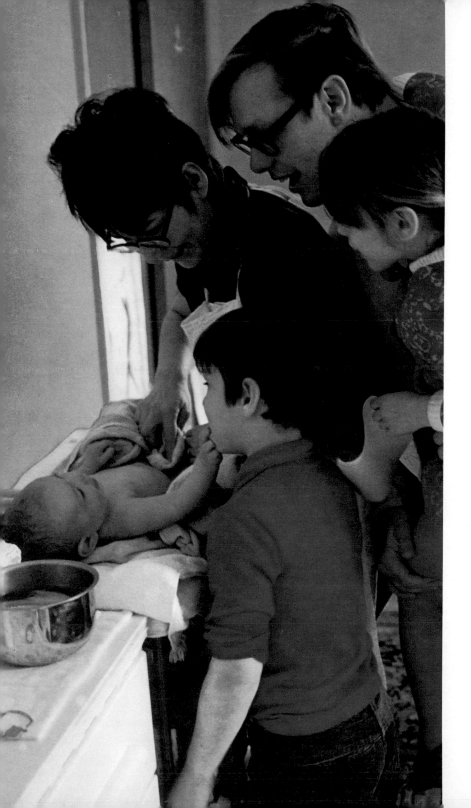

1 The Eucharist
Is About Belonging

My name is

Robert Sottek

**The name
of my family is**

Sottek

**At home, there are people
who love me.**

I love them, too.

Their names are

mom

dad

chris

matt

Robert

How good it is to belong to a family.

Here's a drawing of my family and home.

GOD CALLS SAMUEL

A long time ago, there lived a priest named Eli. He was very old and was going blind. A young boy named Samuel looked after him, and was ministering with him in the temple. Samuel kept the light in the temple burning.

One night when Samuel was about to lie down to rest, the Lord called his name, "Samuel! Samuel!" So Samuel got up. He went to Eli and said, "Here I am. You called me."

Eli answered, "I did not call you. Go back to sleep." So Samuel went back and lay down again. But it happened that the Lord called to him again, "Samuel! Samuel!" Samuel went back to Eli. He said, "Here I am. You called me."

Eli replied, "I did not call you. Go back to sleep." Samuel did not know the Lord yet. He did not know it was God calling him. For a

4

third time the Lord called, "Samuel! Samuel!" Again he went to Eli and said, "Here I am. You called me."

Eli then understood that it was God who was calling Samuel. He told Samuel, "Go back and lie down. If someone calls you again, answer, 'Here I am, Lord. I am listening.'"

So Samuel went back to the temple. He lay down again to sleep. Then God called his name, "Samuel! Samuel!" Samuel answered, "Here I am, Lord. I am listening."

Samuel grew up and the Lord was with him. God stayed very close to Samuel. God made Samuel a great leader of his people.

Based on 1 Samuel 3:1–11

My response to God's word: Here I am, Lord. Speak, Lord! I am listening to your call.

5

When I was a baby,
my mother and father
wanted me to belong to
the Christian family.

They brought me to church
to be baptized.

The priest welcomed me
into God's house.

He asked my parents,

What name do you give
your child?

They answered,

Robert James
_____

Then the priest asked
my parents,

What do you ask of this
Christian community?

They answered,

Baptism
_____

The priest asked them,
Will you bring your child
up in the faith?
Will you help your child
love God and neighbor
as Jesus showed us?

My parents answered,
Yes, we will.

Then I was baptized.

I will rejoice and be glad.
I belong to the Christian family

God knows me
by my name and loves me.

As a mother and father
care for their child,
God cares for me.

I am very special. I belong to
the Christian family.

God says,

I have called you by your name,
and you are mine.

Based on Isaiah 43:1

God has chosen you as beloved children. Therefore love one another. Be always united. For you are called to become one people. Let the peace of Christ live in your hearts. Always be thankful.

Based on Colossians 3:12–15

Happy are those who belong to God's family.

This is a picture of what I see when someone is baptized.

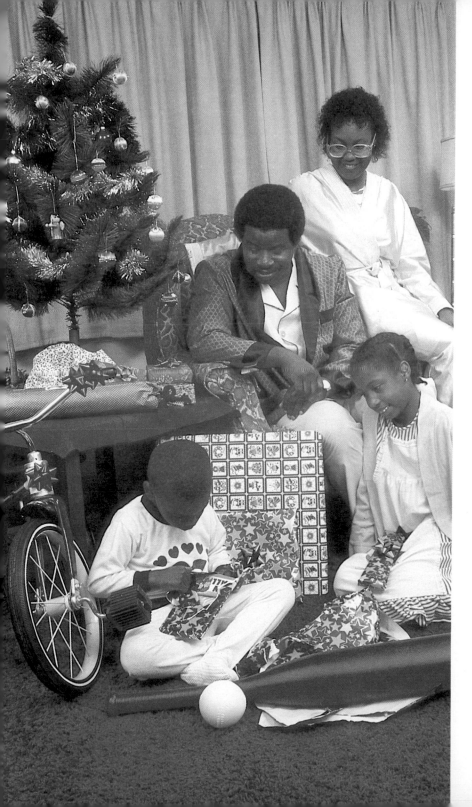

2 The Eucharist Is About Celebrating

11

My family loves to
have celebrations on
special days.

On those days
we invite special
people to our home.

On my birthday
I would like to invite

Remus

Laver

Rax

God gives us a special day
every week to celebrate.

It is called

Sunday

On Sunday my family does
special things.

Here are some of them.

partey

Happy are those who love to celebrate life.

This is my drawing of a celebration I liked.

JESUS IS INVITED TO A WEDDING

One day there was a wedding celebration in a town called Cana. Mary, the mother of Jesus, was there. Jesus was also there with some of his friends.

When there was no wine left for the rest of the celebration, Mary, the mother of Jesus, went to him and said, "Son, they have no more wine." Jesus answered, "Please, do not ask me to do anything about it now. My hour has not come yet." But Mary said to those serving, "Do whatever he tells you."

There were six very large stone water jars nearby. Jesus said to those who were serving, "Fill the jars with water." They filled them to the brim. Jesus told them, "Pour some out now and take it to the head waiter."

The head waiter tasted the water that had now become wine. He had no idea where the wine had come from. He then called the bridegroom and said, "Most people serve their best wine first. They save the cheaper wine until the guests have been drinking awhile. You have saved the best wine until the end of the celebration."

This is the first wonderful sign that Jesus gave to his friends. His friends began to believe in him.

When the celebration was over, Jesus, his mother, and his friends went down to Capernaum and stayed there for a few days.

Based on John 2:1–11

My response to God's word: I rejoice when we go to the house of the Lord and celebrate the Lord's day.

15

There is a special house
in my neighborhood.

We call it a church.

Many men, women, and
children gather there to
celebrate as a community.

They pray and sing
to the Lord Jesus.

Jesus says,

Where two or three come together
in my name, I am there with them.

Based on Matthew 18:20

Glory to God in the highest,
and peace to his people
on earth.

Lord, God, heavenly King,
almighty God and Father,
we worship you,
we give you thanks,
we praise you for your glory.

Lord Jesus Christ,
only Son of the Father,

Lord, God, Lamb of God,
you take away the sin
of the world:
have mercy on us:
you are seated at the right hand
of the Father:
receive our prayer.

For you alone are the Holy One,
you alone are the Lord,
you alone are the Most High,
Jesus Christ,
with the Holy Spirit,
In the glory of God the Father.
Amen.

17

Every week Jesus invites us
to come to a celebration
in God's house.

We are Jesus'
sisters and brothers.
We gather together
as one family.

We come together
to worship God
who is always with us.

This is the day of the Lord.
Rejoice and be glad
when they say to you,
Let us go to God's house!

Based on Psalm 122:1

Here are the names
of some of the people
who join me in the
celebration.

Chris

Matt

mam

dad

Robert

se who celebrate
of the Lord.

Robert mom dad Chris Matt

Here I am with my family
in god's house.

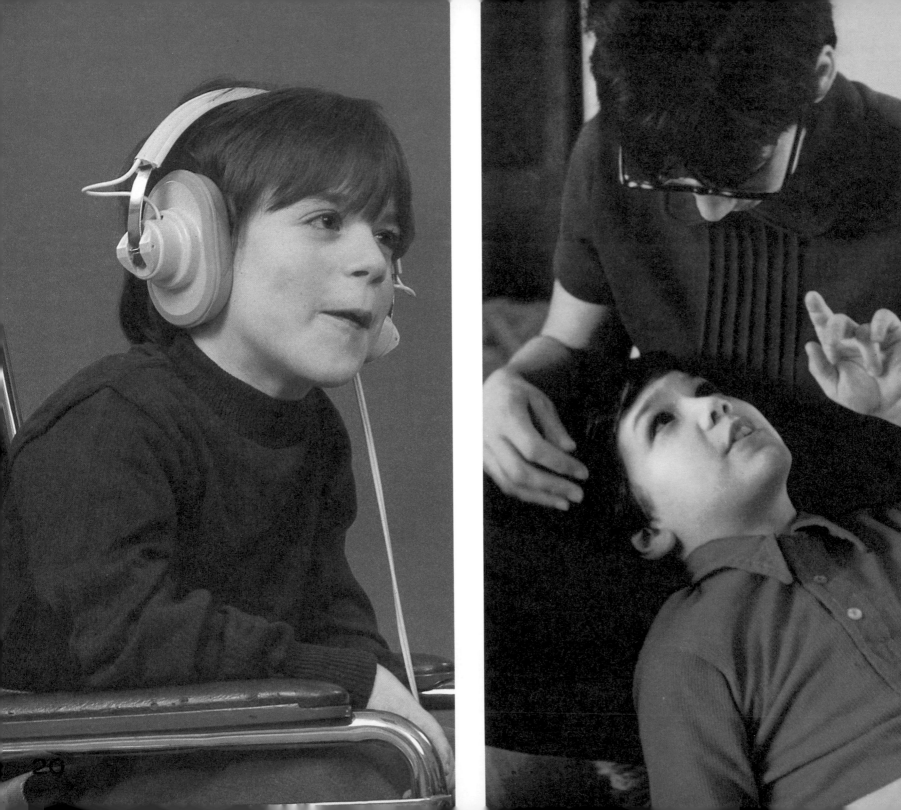

Robert

3 The Eucharist
Is About Listening

There are some sounds
I like to listen to.

There are some voices
I like to hear.

At home I like to listen
to the sound of

my baby brother

On my street I like to listen
to the sound of

cars

At school I like to listen
to the sound of

playing

I also like to listen
to the sound of

base ball

asage

Happy are those who listen well.

my freid

Here is someone I like to listen to.

MARY LISTENS TO JESUS

One day, Jesus was on a journey. He came to a village where two sisters, Martha and Mary, lived.

Martha welcomed Jesus into their home. Her sister, Mary, sat down with Jesus and listened to all he was saying. Martha, instead, was very busy with all the work that had to be done.

Martha said to Jesus, "Lord, do you not care that my sister is leaving me to do all the serving myself? Please tell her to help me."

24

Jesus answered, "Martha, Martha, you worry about so many things. They are important. But the most important thing is to be with me and to listen to my words. Mary has chosen to listen to my words. That shall not be taken away from her."

Based on Luke 10:38–42

My response to God's word: Lord, open my ears and my heart to your words.

25

The Bible teaches us
the story of God's people.

At the Eucharist we listen
carefully to words from the
Bible.

In the Old Testament
the prophets tell us
how God loved us and
promised to send a savior.

To respond to this message
of love we often sing a psalm.

In the New Testament
the first Christians tell us
how to live the
teachings of Jesus.

The gospel teaches us about
Jesus, God's Son.

Jesus lived with us.
He showed us how much
God loves us.
This is the "good news."

To welcome the good news
we stand and sing:

Alleluia, Alleluia, Alleluia!

Happy are they who hear the
word of God.

Jesus says,

If you hear the word of God
and do it, you are my friends
and true members of my family.

Based on Luke 8:21

Here are some words of Jesus that I remember.

Jesus showes us

howmuch God

loves us

John, a good friend of Jesus, calls Jesus the Word of God.

Jesus also gives us other ways to know him better.

He tells us:

I am the bread of life.

I am the light of the world.

I am the good shepherd.

I am the resurrection and the life.

I am the way, and the truth, and the life.

I am the true vine.

Taken from
The Gospel According to John

28

Happy are those who listen to God's word.

This is god's family listening to his word.

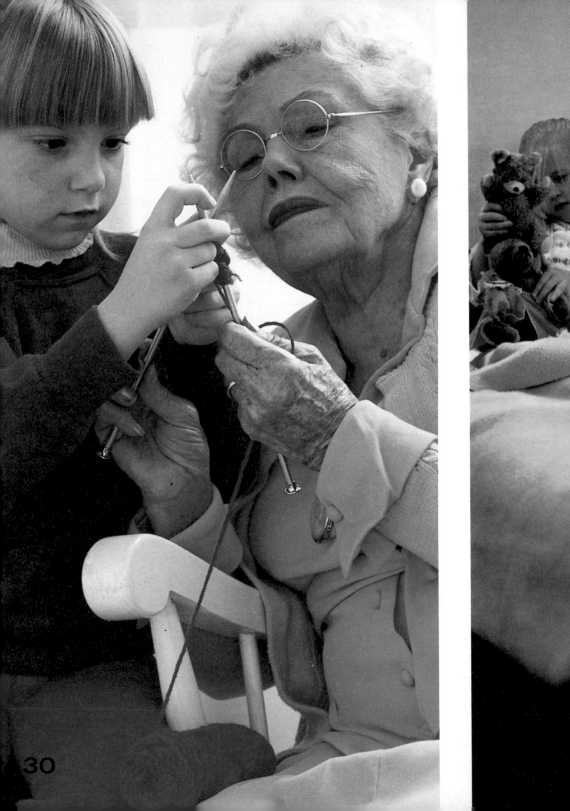

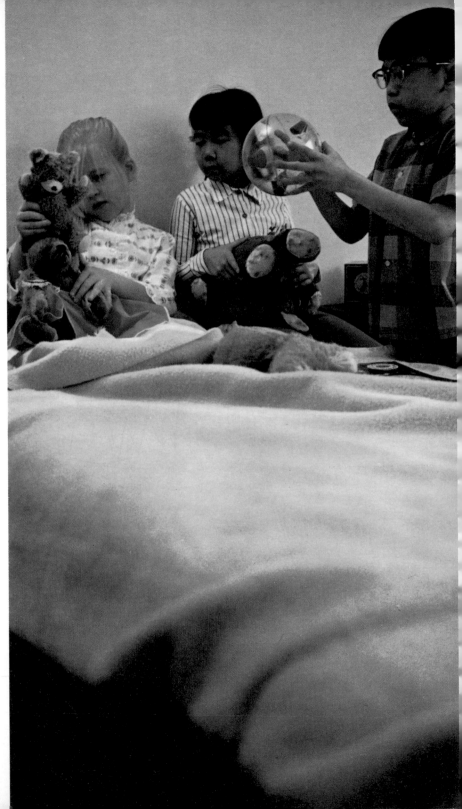

4 The Eucharist
Is About Caring

Many people care for me
at home, at school,
and in my neighborhood.

Here are some people
who care for me.

my neihhbor

emma my freids

bad mom   to
my brothers

I care for people, too.
Here are some things I do
to show I care.

help people

shale

Are there other times
when I can help?

What can I do
when someone is left out
of a game?

let he join

when someone feels lonely?

play with them

when someone feels sad?

chir them up

when someone is sick?

pray for them

32

Happy are those who care for people.

Here are some people who need love and care.

JESUS CARES FOR A PARALYZED MAN

When Jesus returned to Capernaum word went around that he was back home. Many people came to the house where Jesus was staying to hear him speak. The house was very crowded. There was no room left, even in front of the door.

While Jesus was teaching, four men arrived carrying a man on a stretcher. The man on the stretcher was paralyzed and could not walk. His friends wanted him to meet Jesus. They could not get in through the door because of the crowd, so they climbed up onto the roof. They made an opening in the roof, and lowered the stretcher into the house.

Jesus saw how much they trusted and believed in him. He said to the paralyzed man, "My friend, your sins are forgiven."

Some people who were sitting there had a hard time understanding that Jesus could forgive sins. They believed that only God can forgive sins.

Jesus knew what they were thinking. He said to them, "If I can heal this man and make him walk again, will you believe that I can forgive his sins as well?" Then Jesus said to the man, "Stand up, my friend. Pick up your stretcher and go home." The man got up at once, picked up his stretcher, and walked out in front of everyone.

Everyone who was there saw what had happened and praised God. They said, "We have never seen anything like this."

Based on Mark 2:1–12

My response to God's word: Lord, help me find ways to care for those who need me.

35

In God's family
we pray for one another
at the celebration
of the Eucharist.

We call this the Prayer
of the Faithful.

Prayer of the Faithful

For God's family
all over the world,

For the leaders
of God's family,

For the leaders
of our country,

For our parents and
our teachers,

For our friends and
neighbors,

For those who have no work,

For those who have no home,

For those who have no food,

For those who are sick,

For those who are old,

For those who are alone,

For those who are in prison,

For those who suffer from war,

Lord, hear our prayer.

Jesus says,

Happy are those who
share with others.

Happy are those who
comfort others.

Happy are those who
are gentle and kind.

Happy are those who
treat others fairly.

Happy are those who
forgive others.

Happy are those who
love God.

Happy are those who
make peace.

Happy are those
who are faithful.

Based on Matthew 5:3–11

I know people who try
to put these words of Jesus
into practice.

Here are their names
and what they do.

my freids
treats me well
my mother
pray for me

Happy are those who open their hearts to people in need.

These **are** people I want to pray for.

5 The Eucharist
Is About Making Peace

It is often hard to share,
to play with everybody,
to forgive,
and to make peace.

Sometimes I do not get along
with my parents,
my brothers and sisters.

What can I do about it?

make up
forgive one
another

Sometimes I do not get along
with others.

What can I do about it?

play with him

Happy are those who make peace.

Here I am making up after a quarrel.

A FATHER AND SON MAKE PEACE

One day Jesus told this story. There was a man who had two sons. The younger son said to his father, "Let me have my share of our property now." So the father divided the property between his two sons.

A few days later the younger son packed all he had and left home. He went to a far away country and wasted all his money. There was a famine in that country and he became hungry and cold.

A local farmer hired him to feed pigs. The young man was so hungry that he would gladly have eaten the husks the pigs ate. But no one offered him anything.

When he came to his senses, he said to himself, "The people who work for my father have more than enough food, and here I am starving to death. I am going back home. I will tell my father how sorry I am." So he started home.

While he was still a long way off, his father saw him coming. The father ran out to meet his son. He took him in his arms and kissed him.

The young son began to say, "Father, I have sinned against heaven and you. I am no longer worthy to be called your son." But his father said to his servants, "Quick! Bring out the best clothing and sandals. Prepare a meal. Let us celebrate! My son was dead and has come back to life. He was lost, and has been found." And they began the celebration.

Based on Luke 15:11–24

My response to God's word: Lord, help me to forgive others. Help me always to come back to you so that I can be forgiven.

45

In God's family we ask for
God's forgiveness
and peace.

We ask for God's forgiveness
and peace at the
celebration of the Eucharist.

Lord, have mercy.
Christ, have mercy.
Lord, have mercy.

We give one another
the sign of peace.

The peace of the Lord
be with you always.

With John the Baptist,
we say,

Lamb of God, you take away
the sins of the world:
Have mercy on us.

Jesus teaches us
how to pray:

Our Father,
who art in heaven,
hallowed be thy name;

thy kingdom come;
thy will be done on earth
as it is in heaven.

Give us this day
our daily bread;
and forgive us our trespasses
as we forgive those
who trespass against us;

and lead us not
into temptation,
but deliver us from evil.

For the kingdom, the power,
and the glory are yours,
now and forever.
Amen.

Based on Matthew 6:9–13

47

The Spirit of Jesus
lives in my heart
and helps me to know
how to please God,
and how to make
others happy.

The Spirit of peace
helps me to see
when I have hurt
someone.

The Spirit of love
helps me to make peace.

Because you are
God's chosen ones,
let your hearts be full
of gentleness and kindness.

Forgive one another
as the Lord forgives you.

May the peace
that Jesus gives
live in your hearts.

Based on Colossians 3:12–15

Happy are those who ask forgiveness and make peace.

Here are people giving the sign of peace at mass.

6 The Eucharist
Is About Giving Thanks for Creation

Prayer of Saint Francis

Praise to you, Lord,
for all creatures!
For our brother the sun,
beautiful and radiant.
By him you give us light.

Praise to you, Lord,
for our brother the wind,
for the air,
and the clouds,
for the clear sky,
and for every kind of
weather.

Praise to you, Lord,
for our sister the water.
She is so useful,
so precious, and so pure.

Praise to you, Lord,
for our brother the fire.
He is handsome,
joyous, and strong.
By him you make us warm;
by him you light up
the night.

Praise to you, Lord,
for our mother the earth.
She carries us
and feeds us.
She gives us her plants
and her colorful fruits.

All creatures, bless the Lord!

Happy are those who give thanks for creation.

Here are some of God's gifts to me.

THE POEM OF CREATION

In the beginning, God created the heavens and the earth.

God said, "Let there be light!" And there was light. God called the light day, and the darkness night. Evening and morning came. And God saw that it was good.

Then God said, "Let there be dry land and water around the land!" God called the dry land earth and the water sea. Evening and morning came. And God saw that it was good.

Then God said, "Let the earth produce plants and trees that bear all kinds of fruit!" And so it was. Evening and morning came. And God saw that it was good.

Then God said, "Let there be a great light to shine over the day, and let there be smaller lights to shine during the night!" God called the greater light sun. The smaller lights God called moon and stars. Evening and morning came. And God saw that it was good.

Then God said, "Let the waters be filled with all kinds of fish. Let the sky be filled with all kinds of birds. Let the earth be filled with all kinds of animals!" Evening and morning came. God saw that it was good.

Then God said, "Let us make men and women in our own image!" So people were created to share God's own life. God blessed them and said, "Take care of all that I have created. It is yours." God looked at everything and saw that it was very good. Evening and morning came. God saw that it was good.

Based on Genesis 1:1–31

My response to God's word: The Lord has done wonderful things for me. Holy is God's name.

The Eucharistic Prayer

The Lord be with you.

And also with you.

Lift up your hearts.

We lift them up to the Lord.

**Let us give thanks
to the Lord our God.**

It is right to give him
thanks and praise.

**God our Father,
you have brought us here
together
so that we can give you
thanks and praise
for all the wonderful things
you have done.**

**We thank you for all that is
beautiful in the world
and for the happiness
you have given us.**

**We know that you are good.
You love us and do
great things for us.
So we all sing together:**

Holy, holy, holy Lord,
God of power and might,

Heaven and earth are full
of your glory.
Hosanna in the highest.

Blessed is he who comes
in the name of the Lord.
Hosanna in the highest.

**God loves us very much.
Because of this great love,
God sent Jesus to save us.**

**If we open our hearts
to his light and his love
Jesus will give us
a new life.**

He makes us children of God.

This is my prayer to thank God for sending us Jesus.

thank you
for sending
Jesus God
and make ine
the world a
better place

Happy are those who give thanks to the Lord.

a church with the priest

Here is how I decorate this page.

7 The Eucharist
Is About Giving Thanks for New Life

Day after day
parents love
their children.

They spend their lives
and time for them.

This is what my parents
do for me.

give me dinner

and play games

with me

give me luach

I, too, can share my love
and my life with others.

There are many ways
I can do that.

Here are some of them:

kiss them

hug them

help them

Happy are those who share their life and **love**.

dad mom my Bothers

Here are people who share their life
and love With others.

JESUS LIVES A NEW LIFE

Early on Sunday morning Mary Magdalene went to the tomb where Jesus' body had been buried. She saw that the stone had been rolled away from the entrance to the tomb.

Mary stood by the tomb crying. Looking into the tomb she saw two angels sitting in the place where Jesus' body had been. The angels asked Mary, "Why are you crying?" She answered, "Because someone has taken my Lord away, and I don't know where to find him."

Then Mary turned around. She saw Jesus standing there, but she did not recognize him. Jesus said to her, "Why are you crying?" Thinking he was the gardener, Mary said to him, "If you have taken him away, tell me where you have laid him and I will go and find him."

Jesus said, "Mary!" Now Mary knew that this was Jesus. She said to him, "Rabbouni!" The word means teacher. Jesus said to her, "Go to my friends and tell them, 'I am returning to my Father and to your Father, to my God and your God.'"

Mary went to the disciples and said, "I have seen the Lord!" And she told them all that Jesus had said to her.

Based on John 20:11–18

My response to God's word:
Alleluia! Alleluia!
I give thanks to my God.
The Lord is truly alive.
Alleluia! Alleluia!

At every Eucharist we do what Jesus did with his friends the night before he died.

During a meal Jesus took bread. He gave thanks and praise. He broke the bread, gave it to his friends, and said:

Take this, all of you, and eat it, for this is my body. This is my life, which is given for you.

Then Jesus took a cup of wine. He gave thanks and praise.

He blessed the cup, gave it to his friends, and said:

Take this, all of you, and drink from it, for this is my blood. This is my life, which is poured out for you.

Do this in memory of me.

Adapted from the Eucharistic Prayer for Children

We proclaim our faith.

When we eat this bread and drink
this cup, we proclaim your death,
Lord Jesus, until you come in glory.

Lord, because you love us,
you invite us to come
to your table.

Fill us with the joy
of your Spirit.

Jesus says,

There is no greater love than to
give your life for your friends.

Based on John 15:13

Jesus gives his life for us.
This is his sacrifice.

The Bible tells us:

Do not forget to do good deeds.
Share what you have. These are
the sacrifices that please God.

Based on Hebrews 13:16

Give your life
for one another. This is the
sacrifice of Jesus' friends.

Happy are those who share in the life of Jesus.

give Xus food
give us Love

Here is how Jesus shared his life
and love with us.

8 The Eucharist
Is About Sharing a Meal

When we share a meal
with others, we share our
life and love with them.

My parents work
many hours to
buy the food we need.

They share their time
and talent to prepare the food
for the table.

When everything is ready,
we sit at the table
and enjoy our meal together.

We thank God
for the food we have
and for the Spirit of joy
and love we share.

How can I bring joy
to the meals
I share with my family?

share my
love and
care

Happy are those who share a meal.

Here's my family eating
a special meal.

JESUS SHARES A MEAL WITH FRIENDS

Two of Jesus' friends were walking to the village of Emmaus. They were talking about Jesus.

Jesus himself joined them on their journey. Somehow, the two men did not recognize him. Jesus asked, "Why do you look so sad? What are you talking about?" One of them answered Jesus, "Haven't you heard about Jesus of Nazareth? He was a great prophet. Everyone saw his great power and love. We thought Jesus was the one who would make us free, but our leaders had him crucified. He died three days ago. Now, this morning, some women in our group saw Jesus. They said he was risen from the dead."

Jesus said to them, "You just don't seem to believe what the prophets

74

have been saying. It was necessary for the savior to suffer these things and to enter into his glory."

It was almost evening when they reached Emmaus. The two disciples asked him to stay with them for the evening meal. While Jesus was with them at table he broke bread, blessed it, and gave it to them to eat. As Jesus did this, their eyes were opened and they recognized him.

When Jesus left, the disciples were so happy that they went to Jerusalem to tell the others what had happened. They told how they had recognized Jesus in the breaking of the bread.

My response to God's word: Stay with us, Lord Jesus. Be with us at each celebration of Eucharist.

Jesus often
shared a meal with
his family and friends

On the night before he died,
Jesus shared a special
meal with his friends
and said,

I have wanted so much
to eat this meal with you.

Today Jesus
invites me to share in
this special meal.

At the Eucharist
we are called to gather
around the Lord's table.

Happy are those who are called
to his supper.

When we see the bread of life
and the cup of blessing, we say
to the Lord,

Lord, I am not worthy to receive
you, but only say the word and I
shall be healed.

We receive the bread of life and
the cup of blessing with many
of Jesus' friends.

The body of Christ.
Amen.

The blood of Christ.
Amen.

We sing joyfully as we go to the
table of the Lord.

I am now ready to share
in the meal of the Lord.

The bread I shall receive
is very special.
It is the bread of life.

Jesus says:

I am the bread of life. If you eat this
bread you will live forever. I will live
in you and you in me.

Based on John 6:51,56

The cup that I will share
is very special.
It is the life
of the risen Lord.

Jesus says,

Take this and share it. This cup,
which is poured out for you, is the
new covenant in my Blood.

Based on Luke 22:17–22

When I receive the Eucharist,
I am one with the Lord,
one with my family, and
one with God's family.

The cup of blessing that we bless
is a sharing in the blood of Christ.
The bread that we break is a
sharing in the body of Christ.

Based on 1 Corinthians 10:16

Happy are those who share in the Lord's meal.

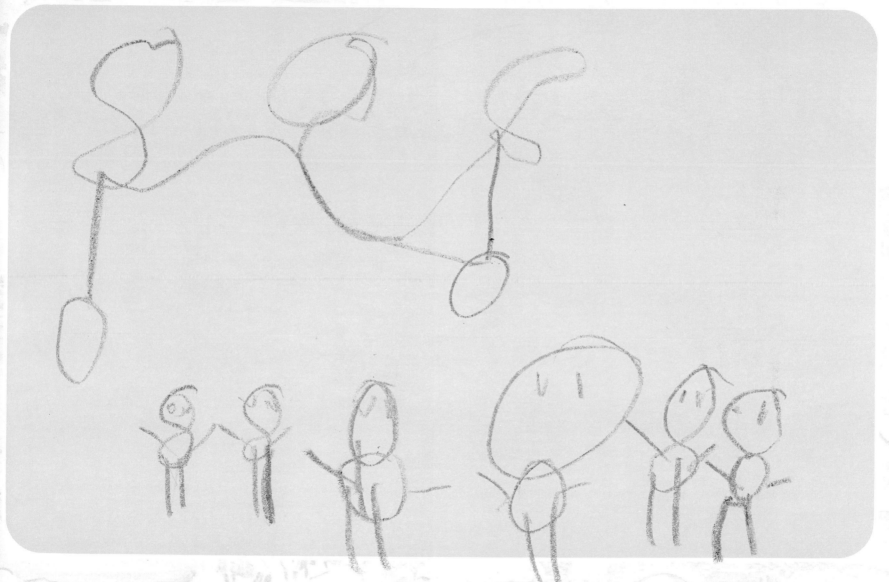

This is how my family and I will celebrate my First Holy Communion.

WE ♥ THE EARTH

9 The Eucharist
Is About Going Forth to Make a Better World

There are many things
we like others to do for us.

What does my family
do for me?

_____

_____

_____

_____

What do my teachers
and classmates do for me?

_____

_____

_____

What do my neighbors and
friends do for me?

_____

_____

Happy are those who bring joy and love to others.

This is how I can show my love for others.

GOD'S WAY TO A BETTER WORLD

One day, Jesus will come again. He will say to those who have lived as he taught,

"Come and receive your share in the kingdom I have prepared for you. I was hungry and you gave me food. I was thirsty and you gave me a drink. I was a stranger and you made me feel welcome. I had nothing to wear and you gave me clothes. I was sick and you took care of me. I was in prison and you visited me."

The people who hear these words
will ask Jesus, "Lord, when did we
do all these things?" Jesus will say
to them: "As long as you did these
things for one of my brothers and
sisters, you did it for me. You have
God's blessing. Come and live
forever in the kingdom which has
been prepared for you."

Based on Matthew 25:34–40

**My response to God's word:
Lord, help me to see you in all
the people I meet.**

After we receive the
Eucharist, we all come
back to our seats.

We keep silent for a while.

The Spirit of Jesus
helps us think of good ideas
for bringing joy
and love to people.

Jesus says,

As I have been sent into the world,
now I am sending you into the
world!

Based on John 20:21

We receive a blessing.

May Almighty God bless you,
the Father, and the Son.
and the Holy Spirit.

We make the sign of the cross
and answer,

Amen.

We are sent forth.

Go in peace to love
and serve the Lord.

We answer,

Thanks be to God.

We leave
God's house with a
joyful song.

John tells us
of a holy city
where God will make
all things new.

In this city
there will be
no more tears,
no more pain,
no more death.

Jesus says,
"Yes, I am coming again,
and I will be with you forever."

Amen. Come, Lord Jesus!

Let us go with joy
to the house of the Lord.

Psalm 122:1

Jesus shall be with us forever.

Revelation 21

Happy are those
who will enter this holy city.

89

A Review
of What I Have Learned
to Help Me Grow
in God's Family

1. When were you welcomed into God's family?

I was welcomed into God's family on the day I was baptized.

2. When we come together as God's family, is Jesus present among us?

Yes. Jesus says, "Where two or three come together in my name, I am there with them."

3. What do we celebrate when we come together on Sunday as God's family?

We celebrate the resurrection of Jesus.

4. What does Jesus say to us about listening to his word?

Jesus says, "If you listen to my word and do my word, you are my friends."

5. When do we listen to the words of Jesus?

We listen to the words of Jesus at Mass when the Bible is read to us.

6. What special name do we use for talking to God?

We call talking to God prayer.

7. Who should we talk to God about?

We should pray for each other, especially for those people who need our love and care.

8. Whom can I love and care for?

I can love and care for my parents, my sisters and brothers, my friends and teachers, and other people who need me.

9. Sometimes we do not get along with our brothers and sisters or our friends. What can we do about this?

We can always try to be better. We can ask God and others for forgiveness when we need it.

10. How does Jesus help us every day?

Jesus gives us his Spirit to help us to know how to love God. He helps us to know how to make others happy. He helps us to make peace.

11. What do we give thanks to God for during the Eucharist?

We thank God for the gift of life, for Jesus, for our families and friends, and all the things we love and enjoy.

12. What did Jesus do so that he could stay with us forever?

Jesus had supper with his best friends. At that supper, which we call the last supper, Jesus broke some bread and gave it to his friends. He said, "Take this and eat it. This is my body, which I am going to give for you. Do this in memory of me." Each time we receive the Eucharist, Jesus is with us in a special way.

13. Is Jesus really with us when we receive the Eucharist?

Yes. Jesus tells us, "I am the bread of life. If you eat this bread, I will live in you and you in me."

14. What do we do after we leave Mass?

We bring the joy and love of God's Spirit to others.

15. What will Jesus do when he comes in glory?

Jesus will gather people from all over the world to be with him in happiness and peace forever.

H I J—McN—96 95 94 93 92 91 90 89 88